easy ANSWERS to awkward QUESTIONS

What 8-13 year-olds need to know about their changing bodies... sex... babies... their rights and more

ILZE VAN DER MERWE & NIKKI BUSH

ILLUSTRATIONS BY RORY MACROBERT

METZ PRESS

Ilze van der Merwe has two children. She is an educational psychologist in private practice with a passion for families. She is a certified Demartini Method facilitator. Ilze is well-known for her popular parent workshop, *How and When to Tell Your Children about the Birds and the Bees* as well as *Powerful Parent Powerful Child* among others. She is a director of Bella Vida in Johannesburg. Visit www.bellavidacentre.co.za for more details.

Nikki Bush has two children. She is a creative parenting expert, inspirational speaker and author on child and parent development issues. She is passionate about helping parents connect with their children. Nikki is highly regarded among parents and educators alike and is well-known for her many dynamic presentations including *Future-proof Your Child*©, *Parenting on the Run*©, *Beyond the Nappy Bag*™ *and Big Kid Fun*™ and more. Visit www.brightideasoutfit.com for more details.

This book addresses a topic which is of a personal and sensitive nature, and the development of the manuscript did not come without its challenges. We would like to say a big thank you to the following people for their valuable input, advice, encouragement, support and fact checking:

- Dr Mark Holliday, General Practitioner (RSA) and former board member of Childline
- Dr Jeremy Baker & Dr Boris Jivkov, Gynaecologists and obstetricians (RSA)
- Dr Richard Godfrey MD (UK), formerly of the World Health Organisation, currently with the humanitarian relief agency Merlin with a special interest in HIV and TB programmes worldwide
- Heather Smith, recently retired principal of Wendywood Primary School where she was also the Life Orientation educator (a portfolio that addresses values, morals, ethics, and life issues such as HIV/AIDS and sexuality)
- Joan van Niekerk, Manager: National Advocacy and Training, Childline South Africa
- Lynne Cawood, Director, Childine Gauteng
- And last but not least, to our editor and publisher, Wilsia Metz , for spotting the gap and making this important book a reality. Thank you for your boldness and for believing in this little book with big impact!

If you are an 8-13 year-old reading this book it is probably because your body is changing or is about to go through the changes of adolescence. We know that this is an exciting time but it can also be worrying if you don't understand what is happening to you and why. Friends can give you some answers, but let's face it, being the same age as you they are unlikely to know much more than you. They may even give you answers that aren't too accurate. Parents or another adult you trust can also be a good source of information — remember, they were your age too once and probably had similar questions.

Because we're involved with parents all the time, we know that some children and parents find it quite difficult to talk to each other about puberty, sex and babies.

This book has been written to answer the practical and sometimes embarrassing questions you've been dying to ask. The answers are straight forward, and are there to help you better understand what is happening to you or what changes to expect when you go through puberty.

In the same way as we lose our milk teeth and get our adult teeth at different times, so every child's body develops at its own pace. You may be an early developer, a late developer or somewhere in between. Regardless of the timing, your body and emotions will go through all the changes explained in this book and you need to be prepared so that you can look forward to your journey towards adulthood with confidence.

ILZE VAN DER MERWE & NIKKI BUSH

Ilze van der Merwe

This book is for my powerful children, Charné and Jacques, who are my inspiration.

Nikki Bush

To my precious, inquisitive sons, Ryan and Matthew, for asking so many great questions! Our honest and sometimes very funny conversations have brought me so much joy.

Published by Metz Press
1 Cameronians Avenue
Welgemoed, 7530 South Africa

First published in 2009
Copyright © Metz Press 2009
Text copyright © Ilze van der Merwe, Nikki Bush
Illustrations copyright © Metz Press

All rights reserved. No part of this publication may be reproduced, stored in a retrieval system or transmitted in any form or by any means, electronic, mechanical, photocopying, recording or otherwise, without the prior written permission of the copyright owners.

Publisher	Wilsia Metz
Design	Liezl Maree, Blue Berry Advertising
Illustrations	Rory MacRobert
Printed and bound by Creda Communications	
ISBN	978-1-920268-27-5

CONTENTS

Chapter 1: Your body has rights too 8

Chapter 2: All about boys 24

Chapter 3: All about girls 38

Chapter 4: Growing up 52

Chapter 5: What's all this about sex and making babies? 74

Chapter 6: How are babies made? 90

Chapter 7: Words you need to understand 110

Index 127

CHAPTER 7

Your Body has rights too

AND MINE

AND MINE

AND MINE

MINE TOO!

Your body

BASICS YOU NEED TO KNOW

You are special.

Your body is special.

Your body belongs to you.

Private parts are private.

You can touch yourself.

You can say no to others.

You must stand up for your rights.

Who to call for help.

has rights too

What makes me special?

Everyone is special and unique in his or her own way. There is no one else like you. The shape of your face, the colour of your eyes and the lines on your hands are just some of the things that make you special. No two people look identical (except for identical twins of course!). Even though you might look like your mom or dad, you are still your unique and special self, with your own thoughts, beliefs, values, personality, talents and abilities. All this makes up who you are.

10

easy ANSWERS to awkward QUESTIONS

Who is responsible for my body?

Your body is special and belongs to you. You are in control of your own body. You must protect your body and keep it healthy. That means that nobody is allowed to hurt, punch, pinch, kick or bully you. You must look after your body properly by eating healthy food, drinking water, giving your body rest and keeping your body clean. Your body must last a whole lifetime so it is important to take good care of it.

Why are private parts called private parts?

Every person has private parts. These are the parts of your body that indicate whether you are a boy (male) or a girl (female). This is also known as your gender or your sex. You will fill out many forms in your lifetime that ask what sex or gender you are: male or female. Private parts are those parts of your body that are

usually covered by underwear or a swimming costume. We all cover our private parts with clothes because private parts are private. This means that they are not to be looked at or touched by other people unless you choose for them to do so. Your private parts belong to you and your private parts are a special part of you.

What are the private parts of a boy and a girl?

A boy's private parts are his penis and testicles and they hang between his legs. A girl's private parts include her breasts as well as an area called her vulva (which includes the vagina) that is tucked between her legs. Your bottom is also considered a private part of your body. Some families have different names for their private parts and that's okay too. You may also hear them referred to as sexual parts or genitals.

Is it bad to touch your private parts?

Touching your private parts is one of the ways in which you will discover how your body works. Your body belongs to you and you have the right to touch yourself. Touching your private parts feels good but remember, private parts are private so it should only be done in the privacy of your bedroom or bathroom, and not in front of others.

Touching or rubbing your private parts is called masturbation. Some people call masturbation playing with yourself. All families, cultures and religions feel differently about masturbation. Some say it's okay and some say it's wrong. However, most doctors agree that masturbation is perfectly healthy and normal. It cannot hurt you or your body.

What if someone touches my private parts?

Your body is yours and nobody is allowed to touch it without your permission. Some adults and children know this but do it in spite of knowing that it's wrong. When grown-ups touch or play with the private parts of children or ask children to touch or play with their private parts, we call this sexual abuse and it is not allowed. Sexual abuse can hurt or feel gentle. Either way, it is wrong. And it is NEVER your fault!

When anybody wants to touch or play with your private parts you have the right to say "NO!". Whenever anybody asks you to touch or play with their private parts, you also have the right to say "NO!". It is also important to tell someone you trust what has happened even if you are threatened or asked to keep it a secret. No one can help you if they don't know what is happening to you.

Always remember that you are special and you have the right to be protected. Say this to yourself often: "I have the right to be protected. My body is mine and nobody is allowed to touch it without my permission".

When can I give someone permission to touch my private parts?

When you were small, you needed your parents or another adult to help you wash your body and to dress you, because you were too little to do these things for yourself. Now you are older and nobody is allowed to touch your private parts unless it really is necessary or if you ask them to.

In certain situations it may be necessary for someone to touch your private parts in order to help you. Here are some examples:

- When a doctor needs to feel certain parts of your body to work out what is wrong with you.
- If you should break your arm or leg you may need your mom or dad to help you wash your private parts when you are in the bath, and dress you.
- If you are very sick and weak, your mom or dad may need to wash your body for you.

Should touching your private parts ever feel uncomfortable, you must tell your parents so that they can take you to the doctor in case you have an infection. This is very important. The doctor may need to examine your private parts to diagnose your condition correctly. This is okay. You may or may not want a parent to be in the room with you. Do what feels right for you.

What do I do if someone touches me without my permission?

If a stranger or someone you know touches your private parts without permission, you need to tell a person you trust immediately, such as a parent, teacher, relative, friend, minister, rabbi or priest. It is important for you to decide what is okay and what is not okay for you. If someone touches your private parts and it makes you feel uncomfortable in any way, you have the right to stop it. Remember that it is your body and you have the right to protect it. Children have adults in their lives to protect them until they are old enough to protect themselves. Therefore it is important to ask for help.

Who can I call if I need help?

There are organisations in South Africa that protect the rights of children. They will help you if you are in trouble:

Childline Toll Free Crisis Line   08000 55 555
Lifeline (national crisis line)   086 132 2322
Crime Stop   08600 10111
Flying Squad (for life threatening emergencies)   10111

www.childline.org.za
www.saps.gov.za
childprotect@saps.org.za

IMPORTANT THINGS TO REMEMBER ABOUT YOUR BODY AND YOUR RIGHTS

✔ Your body belongs to you.

✔ No one may touch your private parts without your permission.

✔ Private parts are private.

✔ Your body has rights — the right to be respected and protected.

All about boys

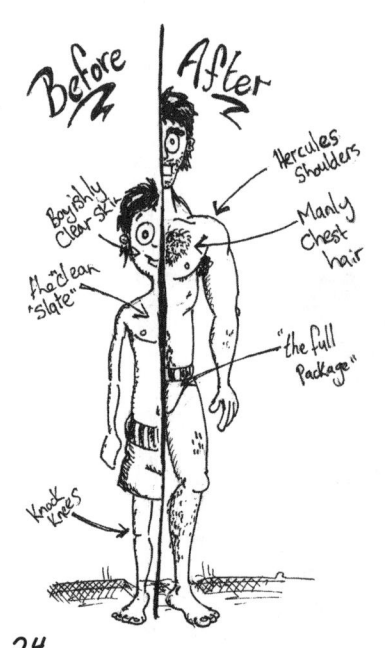

BASICS YOU NEED TO KNOW

Boys have special body parts.

Your body parts have specific names.

Everyone's private parts look slightly different.

Everyone's private parts work the same way.

Boys and girls have different private parts.

Private parts are private.

When you grow up your private parts will change.

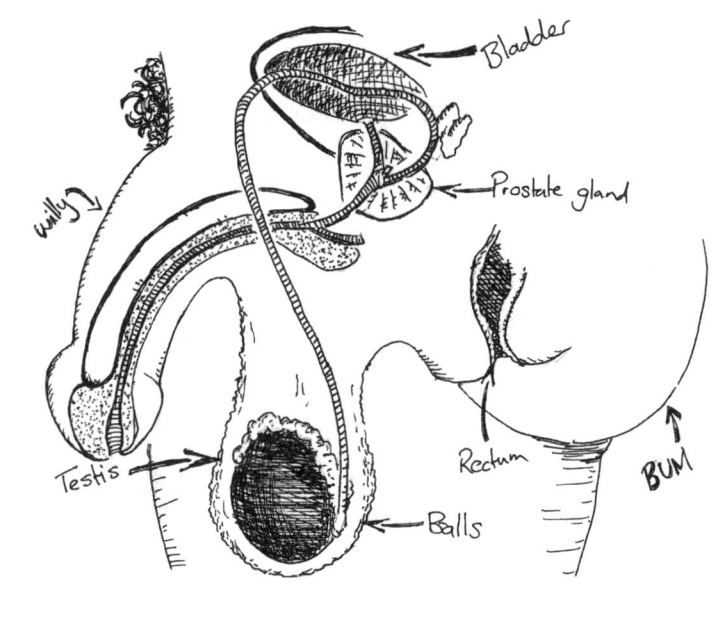

What are a boy's special body parts?

A boy's private parts include his penis and scrotum. The penis is for discharging urine or weeing out of, and the testicles are found in a little bag of loose skin behind the penis called the scrotum. The testicles are where sperm are made. This starts when a boy's body starts changing into that of an adult when he enters puberty. Sperm are microscopic, tadpole-like cells that are important for making babies. Your private parts are special and they need to be taken care of and protected.

Do they have special names?

Just like the rest of your body, your private parts also have specific names. The proper names for a boy's private parts are the penis and scrotum. Some families and cultures have their own names for these special parts. You might have heard some of these:

Penis
 – 'willy' or 'winky'
Testicles
 – 'balls' or 'nuts'

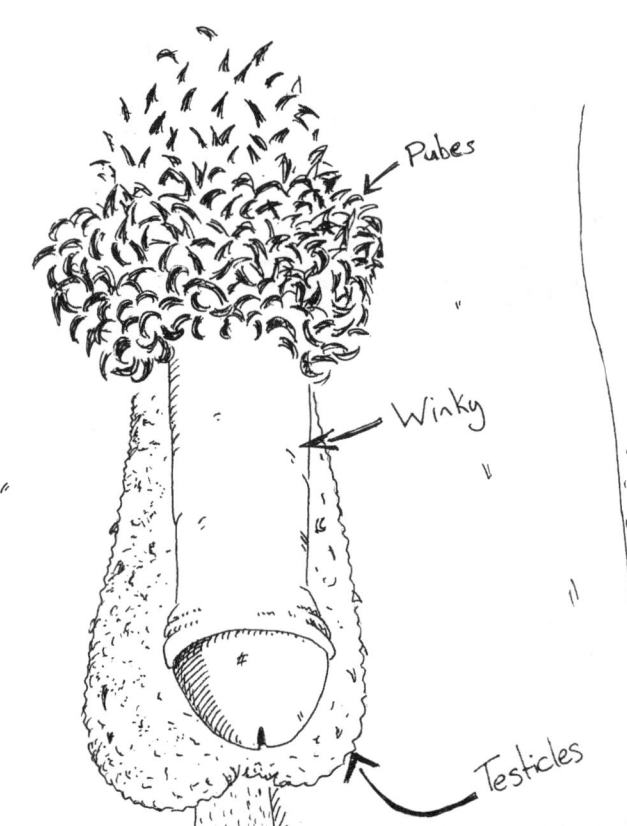

Do all boys' private parts look the same?

Just like his face, each boy's private parts look slightly different. Some boys have smaller or shorter penises than others. It is the same with men. The size may vary but this does not matter. All penises work the same. You will also notice that some boys have a foreskin around the tip of their penis while others don't. This changes the look of the penis but not what it does.

What is circumcision?

Some boys' penises are circumcised. This means that the foreskin around the tip of the penis is removed, usually by a doctor, rabbi or traditional healer. Not all boys are circumcised. In some cultures and religions, it is done to boys when they are just a few days old, in some it happens when they are teenagers who are about to become men, while in other cultures it is not done at all. Parents decide whether or not to circumcise their sons. Sometimes there is a medical reason to circumcise a child, such as the foreskin being too tight, making the penis sore, swollen or infected.

After circumcision, the head of the penis is no longer covered by skin. In uncircumcised boys, the skin can be pulled away to show the head of the penis. Circumcision doesn't make any difference to the way the penis actually works. It just makes a difference to the way the penis looks.

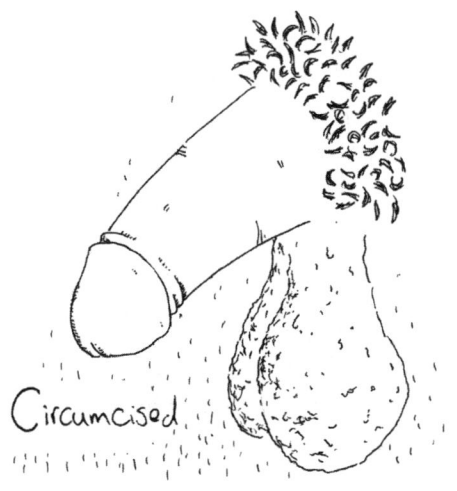
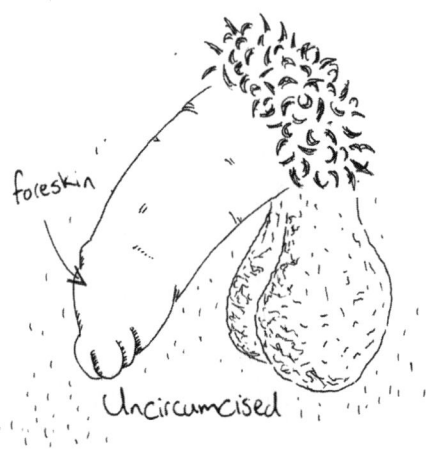

What's the difference between boys' and girls' private parts?

Very simply, a boy has two holes or openings in his private parts and a girl has three. A boy has an opening where solid waste, called faeces or 'poo', leaves his body. It is called the anus. Urine, or wee, leaves his body through an opening at the tip of the penis called the urethra. This opening will also become very important when a boy becomes a man, especially if he wants to make a baby with a woman he loves. It is through this hole that the seeds from a man, called sperm, are released in a white milky liquid called semen. Sperm join with a woman's egg inside her body to start a baby.

A girl has an anus and a urethra too, but she also has a middle hole, which is the opening to the vagina. The vagina is a stretchy tube that connects the outside of the body to the uterus, the sac in which a baby grows. The vagina has three functions:
- It is where the blood comes out when women menstruate.
- It is where the man puts his penis during sex.
- It is where babies come out when they are born naturally.

Now you know why private parts in both boys and girls are so special, and why you need to look after and protect them.

How must I look after my private parts?

A boy's penis, scrotum and testicles should be taken care of in the following ways:
- Keep your private parts clean by washing them regularly with soap and water. If your penis is not circumcised, remember to pull the foreskin back and clean underneath.
- Protect yourself when you play sport, for example wear a ball box when you play cricket. It is made of hard plastic and will protect your penis and testicles.
- Don't let other people touch or play with your private parts. Neither should you allow someone to photograph or film your private parts. Your private parts are private and they belong to you.

Can I touch my penis?

You may have already discovered that it feels nice when you touch your own penis. When we touch or rub our private parts it is called masturbation. Your penis is a very sensitive part of your body. When you touch your penis, blood from other parts of your body rushes into it making it go stiff and hard. The size of the penis changes when this happens – it gets bigger. When the penis is stiff and erect it is called having an erection. It is normal for boys and men of all ages to wake up with an erection. That is how the body works.

What must I do if someone touches my private parts?

It's normal and enjoyable for a boy to touch his penis. Remember, nobody else is allowed to touch your private parts, and you are not allowed to feel another boy or man's penis. When anyone else wants to touch your private parts you must say "No!" Do not allow anyone to touch or play with your private parts. If somebody wants to touch your private parts and saying no is not enough to stop them, this is called sexual abuse. Sexual abuse can be gentle or it can hurt. If you are abused, you must tell a trusted adult who can help you and protect you. Every child has a right to be protected.

Who can I talk to?

When you want to know more about how and why your body and your feelings are changing you should talk to a parent, teacher, relative, doctor or an adult that you trust, or you can read a book like this. Even though children can talk to each other about sexual issues, it is much better to ask an adult as children don't know enough, and some children might even joke about it.

Make sure that you talk to a trusted adult who cares about you and will want to give you the right information. Remember that all adults were curious about their bodies too when they were children. It is normal. You need to feel comfortable about your own body and you have the right to know about it.

IMPORTANT THINGS TO REMEMBER ABOUT A BOY'S BODY

✔ It's okay to touch your penis from time to time, but not all the time, and not in public.

✔ No one else is allowed to touch, photograph or film your penis. It is wrong.

✔ Call for help immediately if someone touches you in a way that makes you feel uncomfortable, and without your permission.

✔ You must look after your private parts to ensure they stay healthy.

✔ Your private parts are special because one day you will need them if you want to start a family with someone you love.

Chapter 3
All About Girls
BOOBS
PUBIC HAIR
HIPS
We get wobbly bits
ALL THINGS NICE
SUGAR
SWEETS
SPICE

CHAPTER 3: All about girls

BASICS YOU NEED TO KNOW

Girls have special body parts.

Your body parts have specific names.

Everyone's private parts look slightly different.

Everyone's private parts work the same way.

Boys and girls have different private parts.

Private parts are private.

When you grow up your private parts will change.

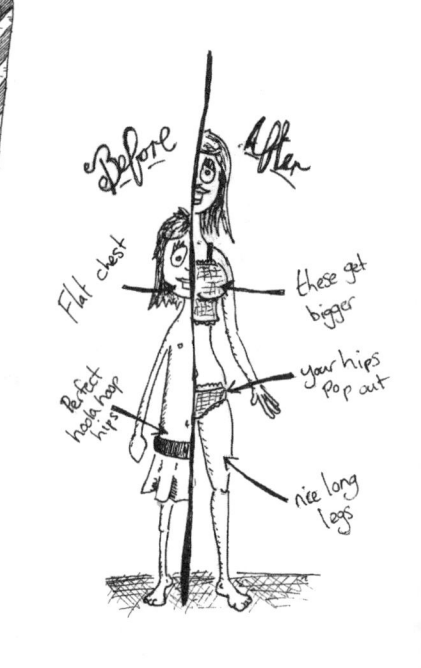

Before / *After*

- Flat chest
- Perfect hoola hoop hips
- these get bigger
- your hips pop out
- nice long legs

What are a girl's special body parts?

A girl's private parts are her breasts and the area between her legs called the vulva, which includes the vagina. Your private parts are special and need to be taken care of and protected. Private parts can also be called genitals. They are the parts of your body that are needed for sexual reproduction when you are an adult. They are what makes a female different from a male.

Do they have special names?

Just like the rest of your body, your private parts also have specific names. The proper names for a female's private parts are breasts and vulva. The vulva refers to the area between a girl's legs. Some families and cultures have their own names for a girl's private parts. You might have heard some of these:

Vulva — 'fanny', 'flower', 'cookie', 'vagina'
Breasts — 'boobs', 'titties'

Do all girls' private parts look the same?

Just like her face, so each girl's private parts look slightly different from others'. You can see a girl's breasts, but her vulva is tucked away between her legs in folds of skin that look like lips and are called the labia. It's a good idea for you to use a small mirror to see what your private parts look like. Every girl's private parts will look slightly different but they all work the same.

Tell me more about a girl's private parts

It's easy to see a boy's private parts, whereas those of a girl are hidden away between her legs. This whole area, from front to back, is called the vulva. The vulva is surrounded by two outer folds of skin called labia, which look like lips. Just inside the labia is another set of inner labia that are much thinner. They protect a tiny bump of skin at the front called the clitoris. It feels sensitive when you touch or rub it. Just behind the clitoris is a small opening, called the urethra, through which urine or wee leaves the body. The opening at the back of the vulva is called the anus, through which solid waste or 'poo' leaves the body. A girl has a middle hole or opening, which boys don't have. This is the opening to the vagina, a stretchy tube which connects the outside of a girl's body to the internal reproductive organs in her abdomen.

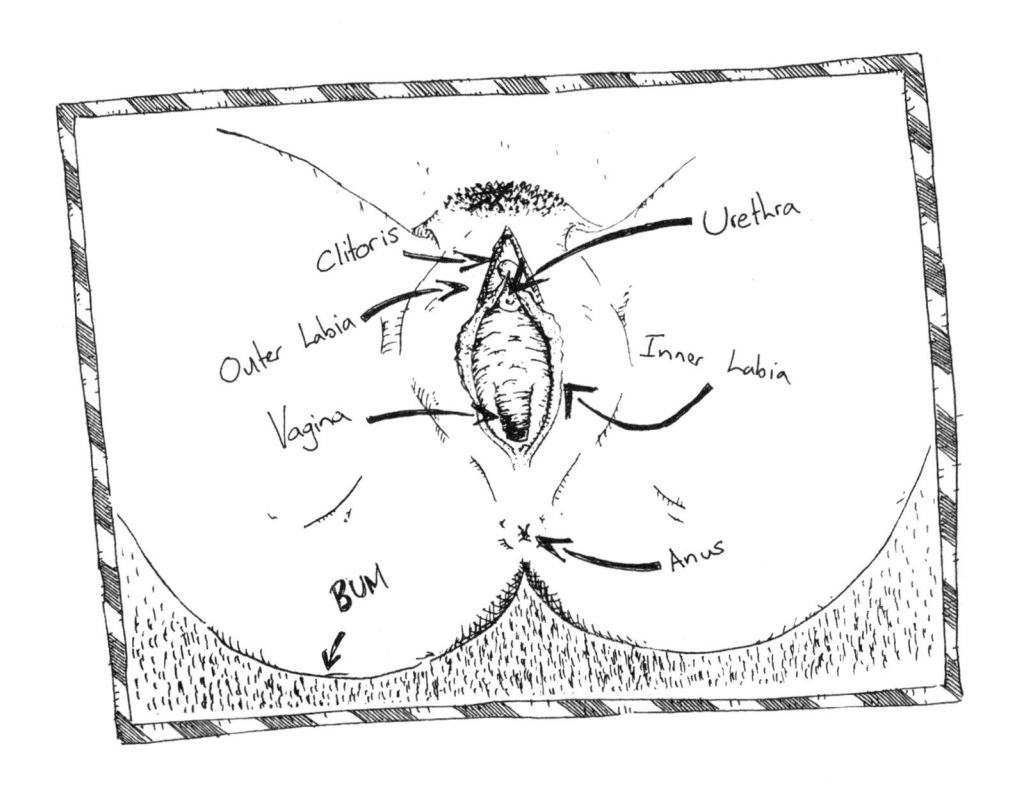

Why is the vagina important?

When a girl becomes a woman, the middle opening or the vagina, becomes very important for a number of reasons:
- A woman bleeds through her vagina for a few days each month when she menstruates or gets her period.
- A man's penis fits inside a woman's vagina when they are having sex.
- It is the opening through which most babies are born (some are surgically removed from their mothers during an operation called a Caesarean).

What are the internal reproductive organs?

These consist of:
- The uterus, which is the special organ in which a baby grows when a woman is pregnant. It is the size of a female's fist.
- Two ovaries, which contain the female's eggs (a girl is born with all the eggs she will ever need in her lifetime).
- The Fallopian tubes, which connect the ovaries to the uterus.

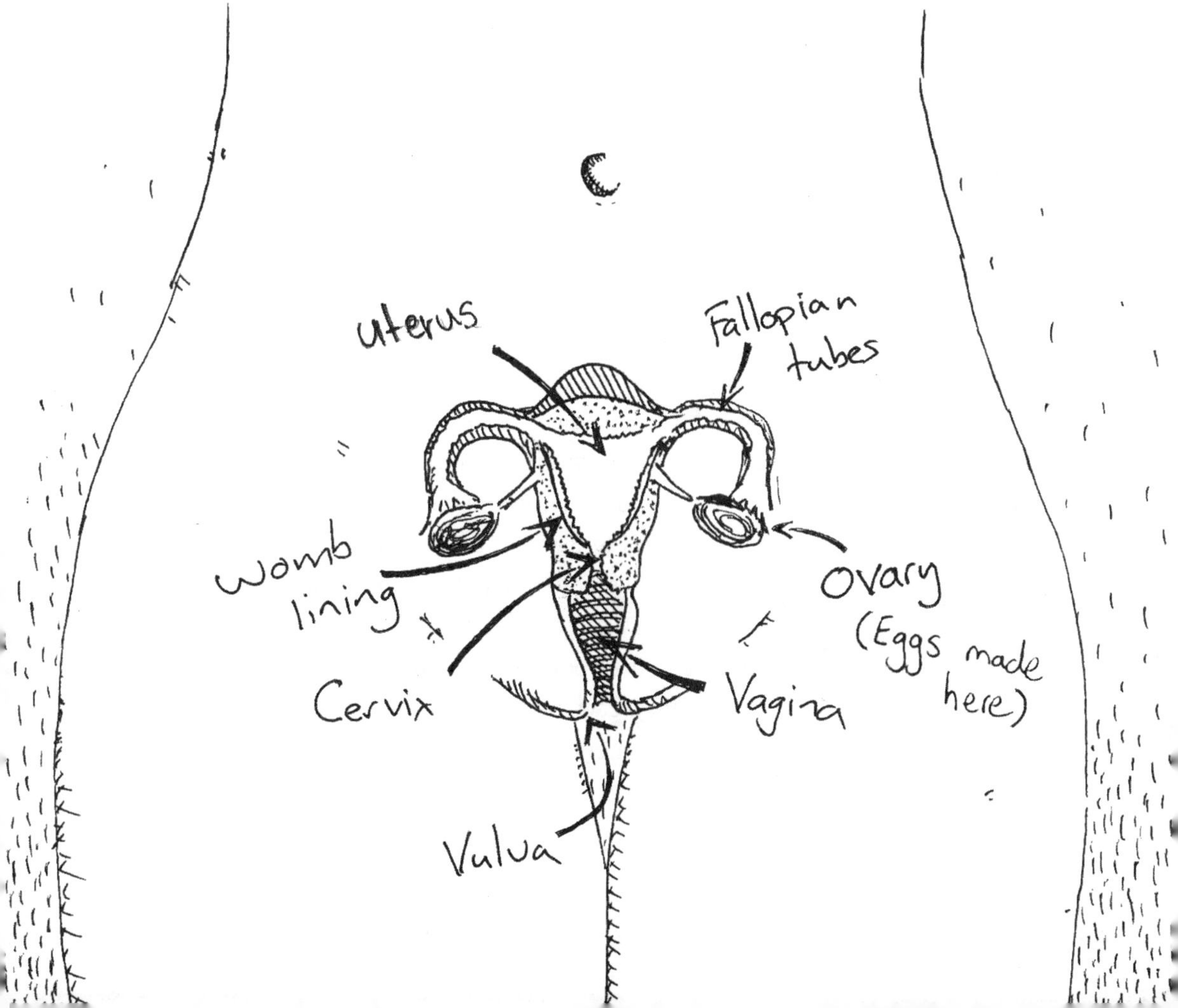

Uterus
Fallopian tubes
Womb lining
Ovary (Eggs made here)
Cervix
Vagina
Vulva

What is menstruation or having a period?

When a girl enters puberty, any time between the age of 9 and 15 years, or when she reaches 45 kg in weight, she will start to bleed from her vagina for a few days each month. This is not because she is ill or injured. It is a sign that she is becoming a young woman.

For a woman to menstruate, she must first ovulate. This means that the eggs in her ovaries ripen and one egg is released each month. The egg is so small it can only be seen under a microscope, and it is released into the Fallopian tube. If it is fertilised by a man's sperm through having sex, it becomes an embryo, or the beginning cells of a baby. The embryo travels to the uterus where it grows and develops into a baby. If the egg is not fertilised, it dissolves in the tube. The lining of the uterus is then released from the body through the vagina. This is known as menstruation, or a period. In this way, the body keeps the uterus healthy and ready for pregnancy. Each month a new uterine lining is formed and another egg is released.

A girl menstruates for three to five days each month. She will use tampons or sanitary pads to soak up the blood and to keep her clothes clean. A tampon is made from very soft, compressed cotton that works like a cork and is shaped to fit inside the vagina. A sanitary pad is a strip of absorbent cotton that lines the panties.

When a woman is pregnant, she stops menstruating.

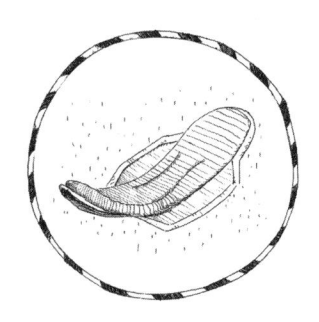

Can I touch my vulva?

You may have discovered that it feels nice when you touch your vulva. Touching or rubbing your private parts is called masturbation. The most sensitive part of your vulva is the clitoris, the tiny bump of skin at the front. It can get quite hard and tingly when it is touched. This is normal and it is enjoyable for all girls and women. Remember that private parts are only for touching when you are alone and in a private place, like in your bedroom or the bathroom. As a child, you are the only person allowed to touch your private parts. One day when you are an adult, and you are in a loving relationship, you may enjoy it when your partner touches your private parts.

How should I look after my private parts?

It is important to take good care of your private parts. Keep them clean by washing them every day with soap and water. You do not have to clean up inside your vagina. This part of your body cleans itself by producing its own moisture. Wear clean panties to protect your private parts. Never push objects into any openings in your private parts. Don't let other people touch or play with your private parts. Neither should you allow someone to photograph or film your private parts. Your private parts are private and they belong to you.

What must I do if someone touches my private parts?

Your private parts belong to you and to no one else. It is important to remember this to avoid embarrassing situations and to keep your body safe from harm or abuse. There is no reason for anyone except you to touch your private parts unless you have a medical condition that needs to be looked at by a doctor.

Remember, nobody else is allowed to touch your private parts. If you are forced to touch another person's private parts or they touch you in a way that makes you feel uncomfortable, or threaten you in any way, then this is called sexual abuse. Sexual abuse may hurt or be gentle but it is still sexual abuse. You must say "No!". Do not allow anyone to touch or play with your private parts. If saying no is not enough to stop them, you must tell a trusted adult immediately so that they can help you and protect you. Every child has a right to be protected.

Who can I talk to?

When you want to know more about how and why your body and your feelings are changing, you should talk to a parent, teacher, relative, doctor or an adult that you trust, or you can read a book like this. Even though children can talk to each other about sexual issues it is much better to ask an adult as children don't know enough, and some children might even joke about it.

Make sure that you talk to a trusted adult who cares about you and will want to give you the right information. Remember that all adults were curious about their bodies too when they were children. It is normal. You need to feel comfortable about your own body and you have the right to know about it.

IMPORTANT THINGS TO REMEMBER ABOUT A GIRL'S BODY

✔ Only a woman can have a baby because she has a uterus.

✔ Never push any foreign objects into the openings of your private parts.

✔ Keep your private parts clean and speak to an adult should you experience any burning, itching or a smell in that area.

✔ It's okay to touch your vulva from time to time, but not all the time.

✔ No one else is allowed to touch your vulva.

✔ Call for help immediately if someone touches you in a way that makes you feel uncomfortable and without your permission.

✔ Your private parts are special because one day you will need them if you want to start a family with someone you love.

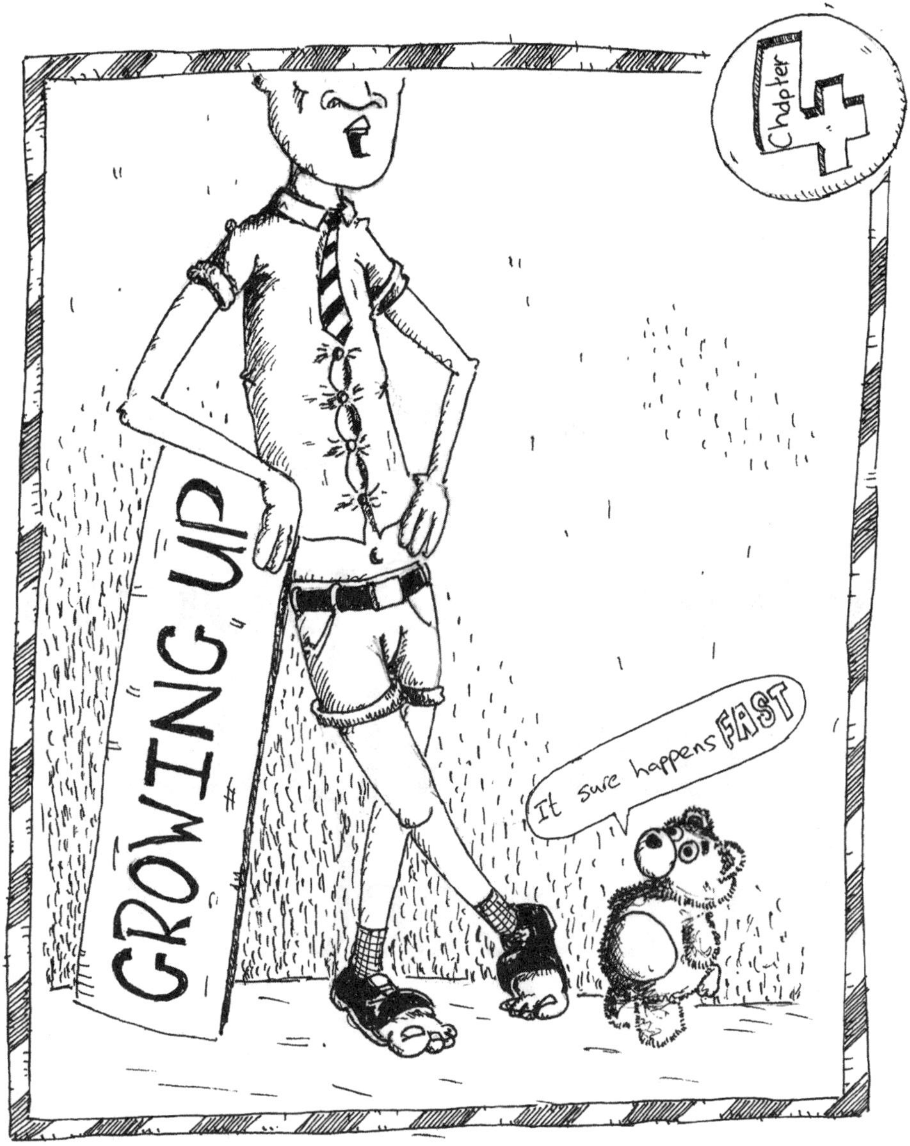
Chapter 4
GROWING UP
It sure happens FAST

CHAPTER 4:

Growing up – what happens and what to expect

BASICS YOU NEED TO KNOW

As you grow into an adult your body will change.

This time of change is known as puberty.

Girls enter puberty earlier than boys, anytime from the age of 9.

Boys enter puberty any time from the age of 12.

Every child goes through puberty – for some it will be earlier, while other children will be later developers.

Puberty is a time of physical, sexual and emotional growing up and it takes a number of years.

When your body starts changing you will become more aware of your appearance and your private parts – what they look like, what they do and how they make you feel.

You will want to know what these changes are all about.
This is normal.

Growing up is not just about your changing body;
your feelings are growing up too.

Puberty prepares the bodies of boys and girls for making babies.

All these physical and emotional changes are normal.

What is puberty?

Puberty is the time when your body changes from that of a child into that of an adult. Special chemicals called hormones are in charge of the process. They circulate in your blood stream making the changes happen to your body and your emotions. Once your body has been through puberty it will be sexually mature enough to be able to reproduce – to create new life in the form of a baby.

It's an exciting time but it can also be confusing. It starts when you first notice changes happening to your body and ends when you are an adult at around the age of 18. The physical changes are the most obvious ones because you can see them. However, there are lots of emotional changes going on too. These will affect your feelings about all sorts of things from your parents to your schoolwork and your friends, and especially to those of the opposite sex. Your feelings take much longer to grow up than your body does.

What changes can I expect?

CHANGES IN A GIRL

- You grow taller.
- Breasts start to develop on your chest.
- Hair grows under your armpits, on your arms, legs and private parts.
- Your body changes shape, becoming more like your mother's. Your hips will get wider and your breasts larger.
- Your body will release an egg from the ovaries each month (ovulation), which means you are now able to fall pregnant.
- When a girl starts to ovulate she will bleed from her vagina each month (menstruation, or having her period).
- Pimples may appear on your neck, face and shoulders.
- Your body produces more sweat, which may have a smell.
- You will become more moody and emotional.

She's going to be cute

56

CHANGES IN A BOY

- You grow taller.
- Your penis and scrotum get bigger and your testicles start to manufacture sperm.
- You will have erections and wet dreams may start.
- Hair grows under your armpits, on your arms, legs and private parts.
- You will start to grow hair on your face and may need to start shaving around the age of 15.
- Your body changes shape, becoming more like your father's. Your shoulders grow wider and you become more muscular overall.
- Your voice grows deeper and 'breaks' when you are about 13 or 14.
- Pimples may appear on your neck, face and shoulders.
- Your body produces more sweat, which may have a smell.
- You will become more moody and emotional.

Will it be painful?

Whether you are a boy or girl your nipples, and the area beneath them, may get hard and feel tender for a short while during puberty. Girls can experience breast tenderness and discomfort in their abdomen (the area beneath the belly button) when they get their monthly period or menstruation. Talk to a trusted adult if you need some pain relief.

What happens when a girl menstruates?

Menstruation is the word we use when a girl bleeds from her vagina or has her period. This happens to every girl after puberty has begun, sometime between the age of 9 and 15, or when she weighs 45 kilograms or more. This is natural and she is not ill. She can carry on with her normal daily activities including swimming and sport.

For a woman to menstruate, she must first ovulate. This means that the eggs in her ovaries ripen and one egg is released each month. The egg is so small, it can only be seen under a microscope. It is released into the Fallopian tube. If it is fertilised by a man's sperm through having sex, it becomes an embryo, or the beginning cells of a baby. The embryo travels to the uterus where it grows and develops into a baby. If the egg is not fertilised, it dissolves in the tube. The lining of the uterus is then released from the body through the vagina. This is known as menstruation, or a period. In this way, the body keeps the uterus healthy and ready for pregnancy. Each month a new uterine lining is formed and another egg is released.

Girls use tampons or sanitary pads to soak up the blood and to keep their clothes clean. A tampon is made from very soft, compressed cotton that works like a cork and is shaped to fit inside the vagina. A sanitary pad is a strip of absorbent cotton that is used to line the panties.

From the time a girl has her first period she is fertile and can fall pregnant. A woman stops menstruating when she is expecting a baby.

What is an erection and what makes it happen?

When a boy or a man's penis gets stiff, we call it an erection. Many men and boys often wake up with an erection. When a boy enters puberty, he becomes more aware that an erection feels good physically. When a boy touches or rubs his penis, or when he looks at someone he finds attractive, he may have an erection. His emotions are working together with his body. During an erection blood flows from the body into the penis, making it become large, stiff and hard. Erections are normal and a sign that a boy is growing up.

What are wet dreams?

When a boy wakes up in the morning and feels a wet patch in his bed, it is because he has had a wet dream. It is quite normal and is nothing to be embarrassed about. During puberty a boy's testicles start working really hard, making sperm. This is what a man needs to reproduce with a woman when they want to start a family.

Sperm are the seeds in a man's body that join together with a woman's egg inside her body to make a baby. They look like tiny tadpoles and cannot be seen by the naked eye. Sperm travel in a whitish liquid called semen. The sperm collect in the testicles. Pressure builds up and the only way for the sperm to get out is through the tip of the penis. This often happens when a teenage boy or man is asleep, and is called a "wet dream". It is nature's way of getting rid of excess sperm, especially in teenagers and men who are not having sex. Semen is not urine. Urine cannot leave the penis at the same time as semen.

Are boys and girls allowed to touch themselves?

When boys and girls reach puberty they find that they may enjoy touching their own private parts more than ever before. Touching and rubbing your own private parts is called masturbation. This is something that all growing children do from time to time to discover how their body works and feels.

Boys may rub their hand along their penis and a rush of blood into that area makes it go stiff and erect. When semen spurts out through the tip of the penis it is called an ejaculation or an orgasm. It is accompanied by very pleasant muscle spasms in the private parts that make the whole body feel good.

Girls may enjoy rubbing or stroking their vulva, especially the clitoris, which is the bump of skin about the size of a pea, at the front of the vulva. When the clitoris is touched or rubbed, blood rushes to the vulva. The clitoris becomes hard and tingly and the vagina becomes moist. A girl has an orgasm when she experiences very pleasant muscle spasms in her private parts.

Remember that private parts are private which means that you may only touch yourself in the privacy of your bedroom or bathroom. Masturbation is not something you do all the time. It helps you to discover your sexuality. It is good to know how your body works.

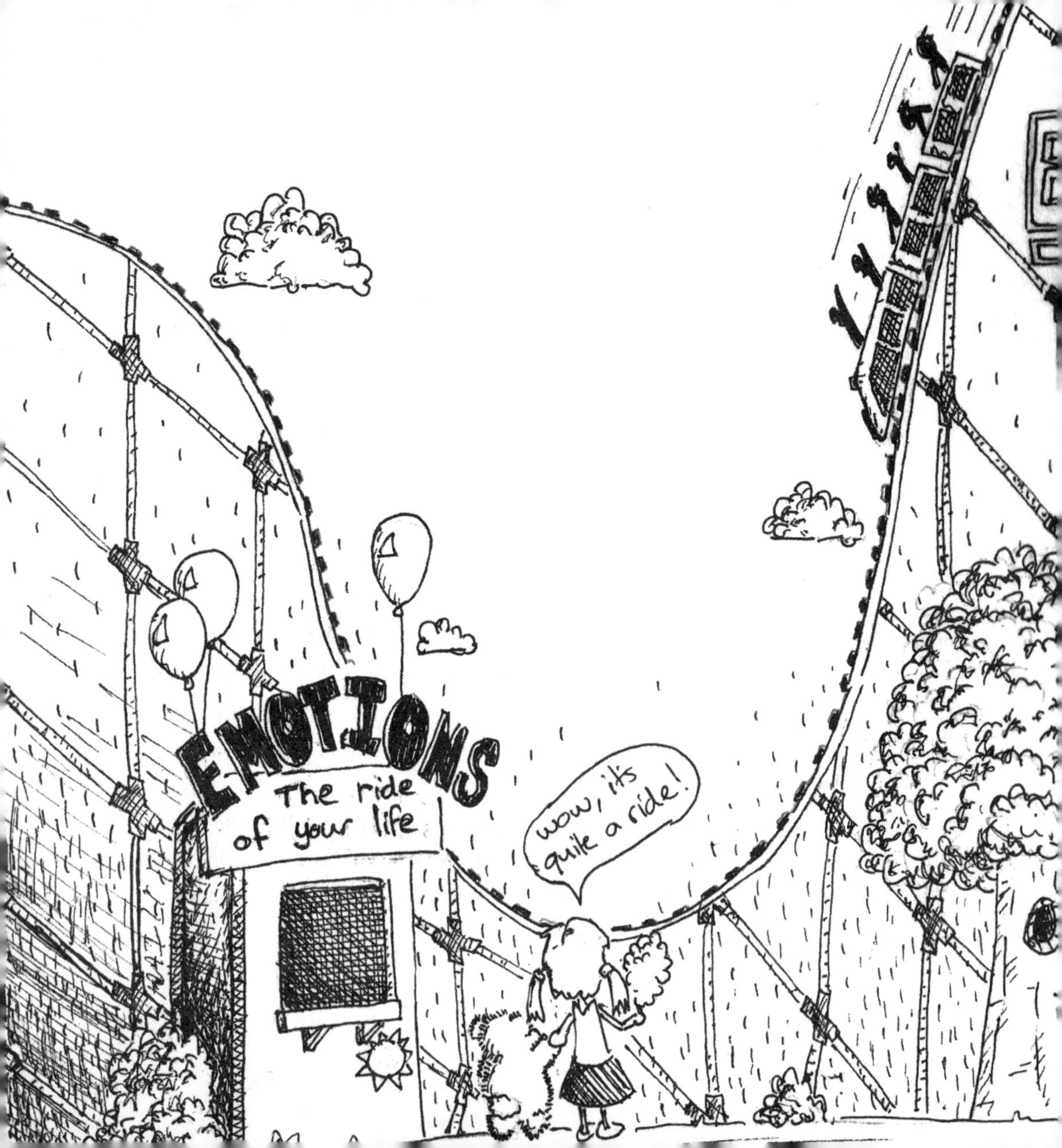
EMOTIONS
The ride of your life
wow, it's quite a ride!

How will my feelings change?

During puberty your feelings will change a lot. You may become emotional or a bit moody and you may experience many different feelings in one day. It might feel a bit like being on a roller coaster – up one minute and down the next. This is normal and is caused by chemicals in your body, called hormones. Your body needs hormones to change you into an adult. It's important to remember that feelings are not right or wrong; it's what you do with them that counts. If you talk to a trusted adult about your changing feelings you will discover that when he or she was the same age he or she probably felt quite similar to the way you feel. Puberty is a time of getting to know and understand your feelings.

What does all this mean?

When boys' and girls' bodies start to change they are on the road to becoming young adults. This is why you are called an adolescent during this time. All these changes will enable a girl to conceive and carry a baby, and a boy to father a child. It is a time when girls and boys start thinking more and more about sex (sexual intercourse) and may often feel attracted to members of the opposite sex. This is normal.

During adolescence you may go through moody patches. This is normal and your feelings may change quickly from one thing to another. You will start to spend more time with your friends who are very important to you. Remember that you and your friends are all going through similar changes, but they may not happen to all of you at exactly the same time.

Part of becoming an adult is learning to understand and control your feelings about all sorts of things, including who you want to be your friends, how you will behave, your attitude towards your schoolwork, your choice of career, having sex and making babies.

What is sex, and what happens during sex?

Sex, sexual intercourse, or making love, is the way in which human reproduction takes place. Babies are made when a man and a woman have sex. However, becoming a parent is something that requires an enormous amount of responsibility and maturity. While adolescents' bodies may be physically mature enough to create a baby, they are not yet emotionally mature enough or financially independent enough to become a parent. This is why sex is something only mature adults should do.

When a man and a woman have sex, they hug, kiss, touch, tickle and rub each other's bodies and private parts. They are usually naked. A man and a woman's body fit together like two pieces of a puzzle. A man's erect penis slides inside a woman's vagina during sex. This is the secret of how the sperm get inside the woman's body to make a baby. When a man has an orgasm he experiences very pleasant muscle spasms in his private parts, which force semen to spurt out of the tip of his penis into the woman's vagina. A woman also experiences very pleasant muscle spasms in her private parts when she has an orgasm. Sex is a physical way in which a man and a woman share their love with each other. It is also how babies are made.

Sex between a man and a woman who love each other is a beautiful and special experience. However, it is not something adolescents should do because sex can have some very serious consequences, which they may not be ready to handle, and that could affect them for the rest of their lives, such as:

- Sex can result in a baby should the girl fall pregnant.
- Sexually transmitted diseases (STDs) can be passed on from one person to another during sex. Symptoms include sores on the inside and outside of the private parts as well as on the mouth; smells, itching, burning and oozing from the private parts. The person feels very sick and is very infectious.
- Sex is one of the most common ways of becoming infected with HIV. HIV can develop into full-blown AIDS, which kills millions of people around the world every year.

Sex is only for adults

Sex, or making love, is not for children. Until you are emotionally and financially capable of looking after a baby, you are not ready to take on the responsibilities that come with having sex. Having to be responsible for a baby when you are only a child yourself, could mean having to leave school early, maybe never even getting your matric or studying for a career you have dreamed about. If you are old enough, you may have to leave school to get a job to support your baby financially. Always remember that sex can lead to pregnancy and becoming a parent unexpectedly, when you are very young, can limit the opportunities available to you when you start your adult life. This is why sex is only for adults.

easy ANSWERS to awkward QUESTIONS

IMPORTANT THINGS TO REMEMBER ABOUT GROWING UP

✔ Changes to your body and emotions during puberty are normal.

✔ The changes that happen to you during puberty are not a secret, they are just private.

✔ These changes happen to everyone at slightly different times.

✔ As your body changes and reaches sexual maturity, you have all that is necessary to make a baby with a member of the opposite sex, but you are not yet emotionally mature enough or financially secure to look after a baby.

✔ Sex is only for adults because it has serious consequences including babies.

✔ Your body belongs to you and no one else. You must protect yourself by getting the right information and understanding what can and does happen when your body changes.

✔ Be responsible about your body and your emotions and you will have a more enjoyable life with fewer worries and complications.

✔ If you need more information ask your parents or an adult you trust.

Chapter 5

What's all this about sex and making babies?

BASICS YOU NEED TO KNOW

Sex can be called many things including sexual intercourse and making love.

Babies are made when a man and a woman have sex.

A sperm from a man's body must join together with an egg from a woman's body to create a baby.

Sex is not a secret, it is just private.

What's all this and making

CHAPTER 5: about sex babies?

Is it normal for me to want to know about sex?

Absolutely! Everyone is curious about sex and how babies are made. We all want to know where we come from. One day when you are an adult and in a special relationship, you may want to have sex with your partner, and you may even decide you are ready to have babies and start your own family. It is very important for you to understand the connection between having sex and making babies!

Sex made you!

That's right! Many years ago, your mom and dad had sex and you were conceived. During sex a sperm from your dad joined together with an egg from your mom, inside her body. A special new baby was formed – you! That's why you have some of your mother's features or characteristics and some of your father's. Now you may be wondering how the sperm got to the egg, and what a sperm and an egg are anyway.

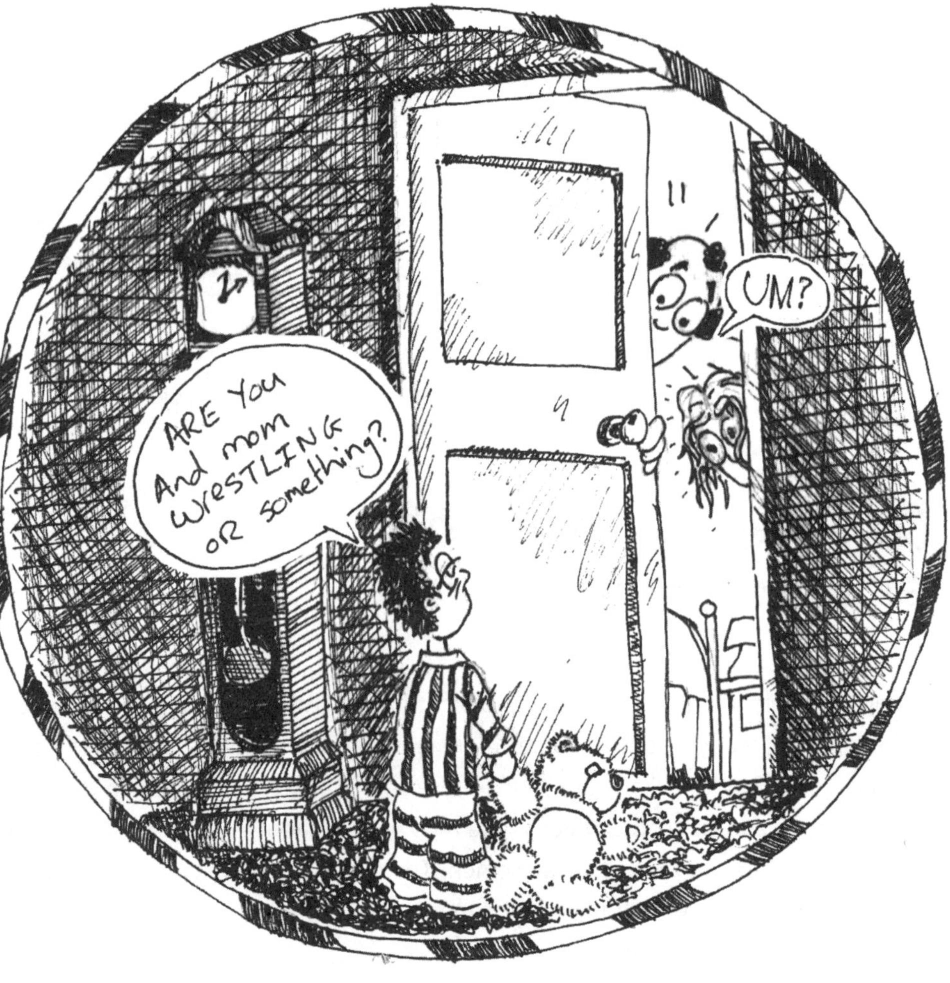

ARE YOU And mom WRESTLING OR something?
UM?

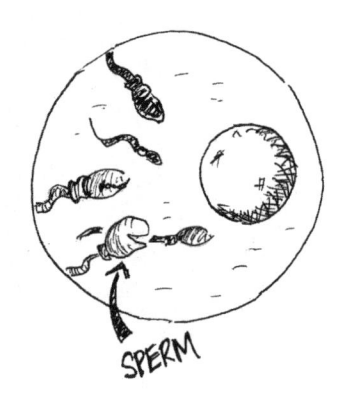

Where do a man's sperm come from?

A boy's testicles are found in his scrotum that hangs just behind his penis. During puberty, when a boy's body becomes more like that of a man, his testicles start to produce millions and millions of sperm. These sperm are so small you can only see them through a microscope, which is like a powerful magnifying glass. They swim around in a white, milky fluid called semen. The only way sperm can be released from the testicles is through the tip of a man's penis when a man has sex, a wet dream or when he masturbates.

Where do a woman's eggs come from?

Inside every girl are thousands of tiny eggs that cannot be seen by the naked eye. Girls are born with all their eggs. They are stored inside two ovaries, which are on either side of the uterus. A baby grows inside the uterus during pregnancy. You can think of the ovaries as an egg incubator inside the lower part of a girl's abdomen.

During puberty, when a girl's body starts growing and changing into that of a woman, her ovaries start releasing one egg each month. This is called ovulation. The egg travels down the Fallopian tubes that connect the ovaries to the uterus.

How does the sperm get to the egg?

During sex, a man deposits semen inside a woman's vagina from his penis when he ejaculates. The semen is filled with millions of tiny sperm that swim up through the vagina, into the uterus, and up the Fallopian tubes inside the woman's abdomen. They are all in search of a single egg. If a single sperm meets an egg, they merge together and the egg is fertilised to form an embryo. This is the beginning stage of a baby.

What happens next?

The embryo travels down into the woman's uterus, which is the special organ in which babies grow and develop inside a woman's abdomen. The embryo attaches onto the inside of the uterus and now becomes known as a foetus. When a woman doesn't get her period (monthly bleeding from her vagina), this is often a reliable sign that she is carrying a baby. We say that she is pregnant.

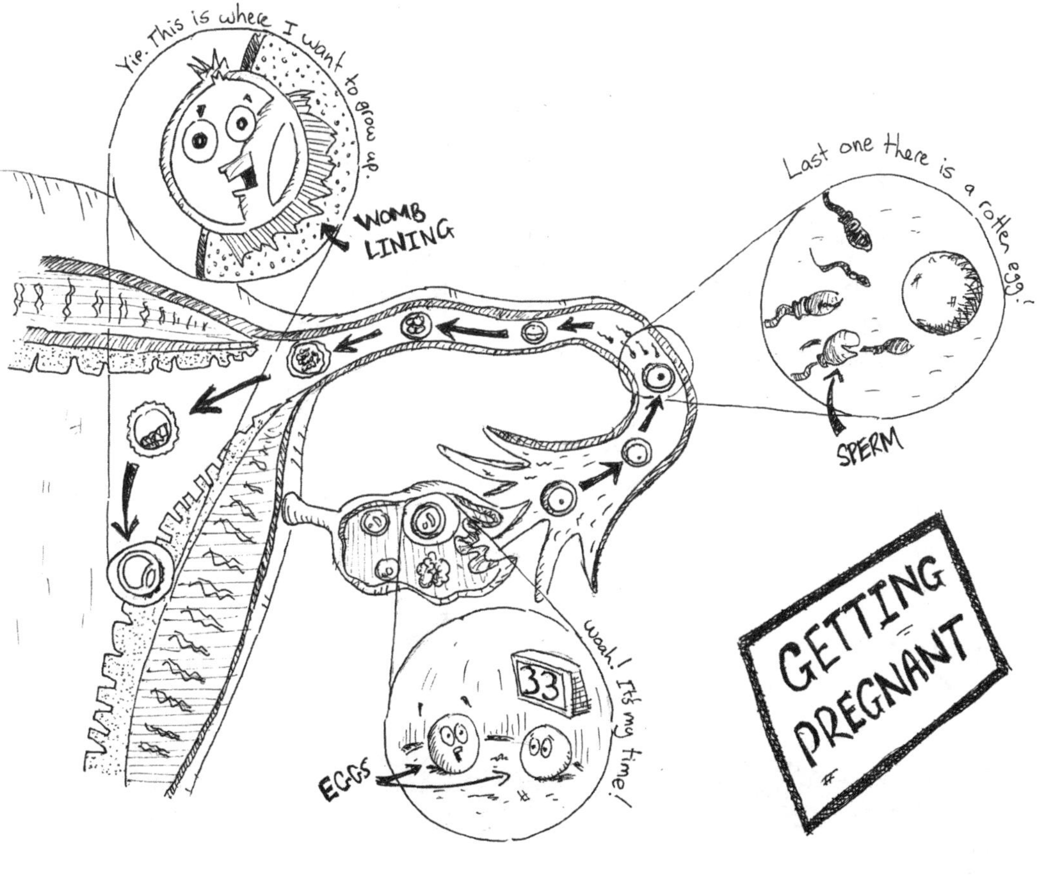
Yip. This is where I want to grow up.
WOMB LINING
Last one there is a rotten egg!
SPERM
Waah! It's my time!
33
EGGS
GETTING PREGNANT

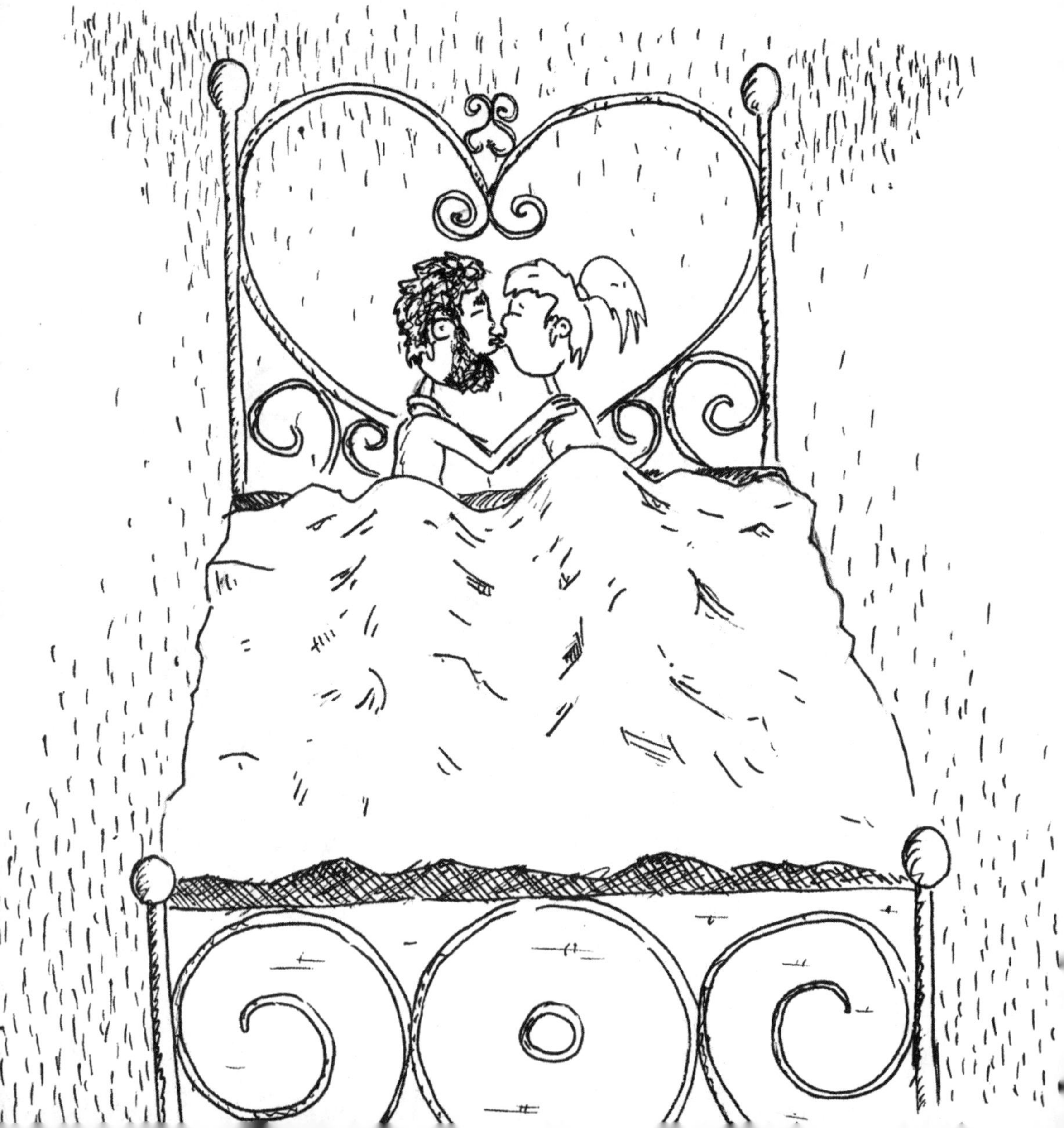

What happens if the egg and sperm do not meet?

Should the egg not be fertilised, it dissolves in the Fallopian tube. Then the soft lining of the uterus gets released by the body through the woman's vagina. This is called menstruation or having her monthly period. This is the way in which the body keeps the uterus healthy and ready for possible pregnancy.

So sex doesn't always create a baby then?

That's correct. In order for a baby to be made, sex must take place close to the time of a woman's ovulation. This is when her body releases an egg from her ovaries once a month. Men and women who feel they are not ready to start a family may use some form of protection, called contraception, to make sure that the sperm and egg do not meet. This is called family planning. You may have heard of The Pill and condoms, as these are the most popular forms of contraception.

Why is sex only for adults?

Sex should only take place between two adults who love each other, who agree to have sex with each other and who are kind and respectful to each other. Sex is only okay between two adults when they both want to share their special love with each other or when they want to make a baby. Adults should only have sex with other adults. It is not okay for adults to have sex with children. This is called sexual abuse.

Sex is not something children do because it can have serious consequences that they are not yet ready to cope with, such as:
- Falling pregnant.
- Becoming infected with a sexually transmitted disease (STD).
- Becoming infected with HIV, which could lead to AIDS and even death.

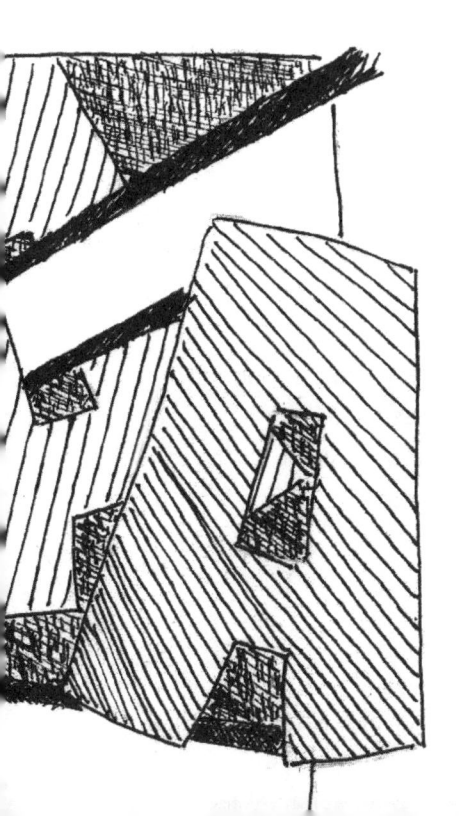

Lots of emotions and feelings are involved with sex and these can be very confusing for children whose feelings have not yet matured or grown up. Sex comes with many responsibilities, such as protecting yourself and your partner from infections and disease, choosing and using contraception and being able to afford to support a child should you create a baby.

People in some cultures and religions believe that they should only have sex if they are married. Ask your parents about your family's cultural or religious beliefs about sex and having children.

Who can I talk to about sex?

Sex is not a secret, but it is private. This is why children and even adults can sometimes be shy or embarrassed when they talk about sex. Parents know a lot but they don't always want to tell their children about sex. Sometimes they need you to ask questions first so that that they know that you are ready to learn about your body and sex. The best people to talk to about sex are usually your parents. If they don't want to, or cannot answer your questions, then ask another adult you trust, like a teacher, nurse, doctor, grandparent, uncle or aunt, or read a book like this.

You will not want to know everything about your changing body or sex all at once. However, as you need to understand more and as you think of questions you would like to ask, speak to a trusted adult who can give you the answers. Trust your feelings to guide you to the right person with whom you feel comfortable, and who has your best interests at heart.

All children are curious about sex, but they don't really know enough to answer questions about sex from other children. You need to know the correct facts so that you understand what is happening to your body when it starts to change into that of an adult, and how to make wise choices.

IMPORTANT THINGS TO REMEMBER ABOUT SEX

✔ Sex is for adults only.

✔ Babies can be made when a man and a woman have sexual intercourse.

✔ A sperm and an egg have to join together to form a baby.

✔ A number of serious infections and diseases can be spread from one person to another through sex. Some of them can even kill you.

✔ Know the facts so that you can protect your body and make wise decisions about your life.

This book is great!

EASY ANSWERS to Questions

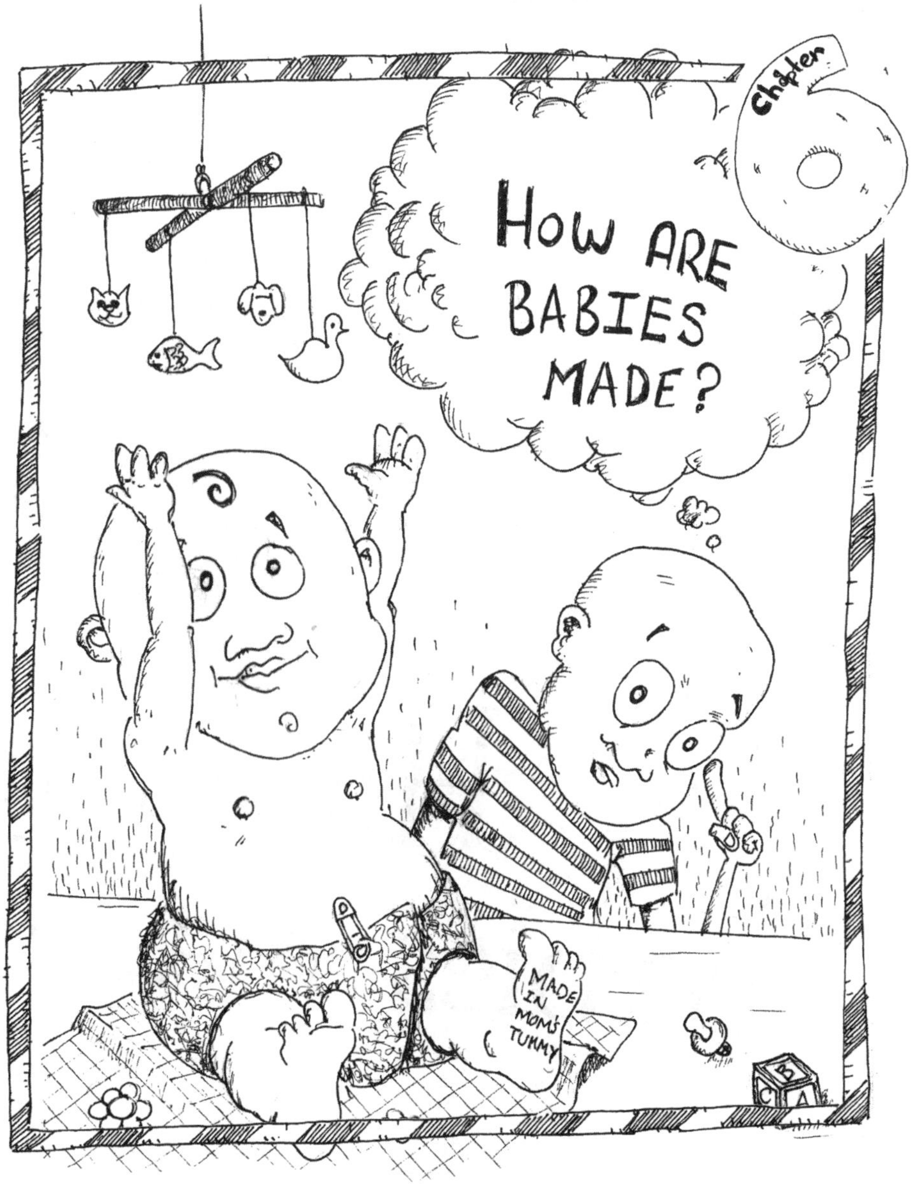

Chapter 6
HOW ARE BABIES MADE?
MADE IN MOM'S TUMMY

CHAPTER 6: How are babies made?

really pregnant!

BASICS YOU NEED TO KNOW

Babies are created through sex between a man and a woman.

A sperm and an egg are needed to form a baby.

When a sperm joins together with an egg we say that a baby has been conceived.

When a woman is carrying a baby we say that she is pregnant.

Pregnancy lasts approximately 40 weeks.

The baby grows inside the uterus in a woman's abdomen.

The embryo starts off the size of a speck and grows to become a baby of 2,5-4 kg.

Most babies around the world are born through a woman's vagina.

When a baby is surgically removed from its mother this is called a Caesarean birth.

How long is pregnancy?

A woman is pregnant with a baby for 40 weeks, or 9 months. It takes this long for a foetus to grow from a little speck to the size of a newborn baby, weighing quite a few kilograms.

What happens during pregnancy?

When a sperm joins together with an egg, fertilisation occurs. This is the moment of conception. This tiny ball of cells doesn't look anything like a baby. After attaching itself to the soft lining of the uterus, it is called an embryo. When the mother is about three months pregnant, the embryo starts looking more like a baby, with a face, body, arms and legs. We call it a foetus. As the foetus grows bigger so does the mother's abdomen.

During pregnancy the uterus is known as the womb. It is a very warm and safe place in which the baby can grow. The womb is filled with warm liquid called amniotic fluid, enabling the baby to move around. From about halfway through the pregnancy, the mother can feel the baby's movements and may even see her stomach move as the baby kicks her from the inside.

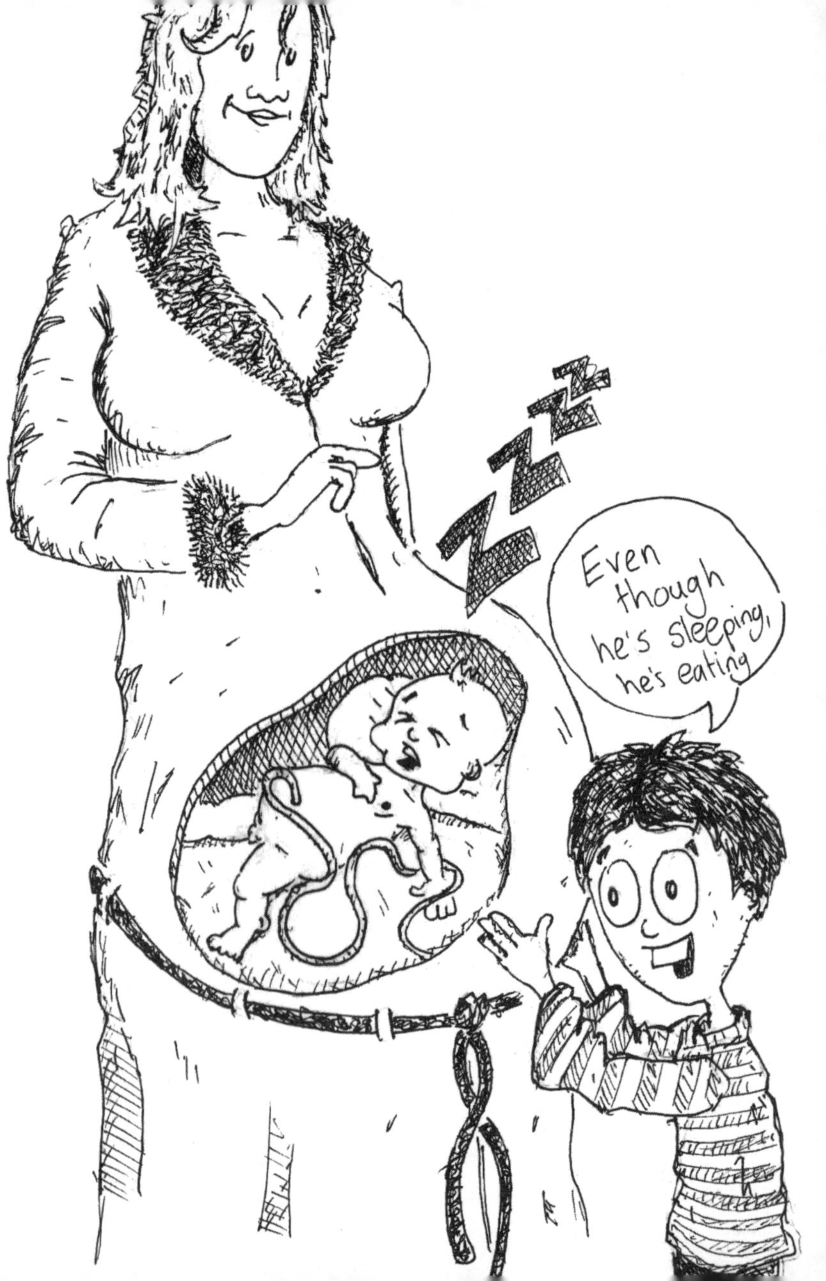
Even though he's sleeping, he's eating

How does the foetus get its food?

The baby cannot survive by itself. Nutrients and oxygen travel from the mother via the placenta, through the umbilical cord to the baby. The placenta is a plate-shaped organ that only develops during pregnancy. It is attached to the wall of the uterus and connects the mother and the baby, providing the baby with nourishment and oxygen, as well as removing waste products. The mother's body releases the placenta a few minutes after the baby's birth. When the baby is born, the umbilical cord is cut and the remaining stump dries within a few days, falls off and becomes the belly button. Your belly button is the place where your body was attached to your mother.

Every second that a foetus is inside its mother's body it is growing. All parts of the baby's body develop over the 40 weeks of pregnancy until it has every organ (for example the heart), every body part (for example arms), and every sensory organ (for example eyes) to ensure it will survive outside the womb when it is born.

How does the baby stay in?

The bottom of the womb is kept closed by the woman's cervix. This is a tiny, stretchy opening that remains very tightly shut during the 40 weeks of pregnancy. It has a small plug made of a jelly-like substance that stays in place for the whole pregnancy ensuring that none of the amniotic fluid leaks out. When the baby is ready to be born, the plug pops out and the cervix expands like an elastic band to let the baby travel out through a woman's vagina.

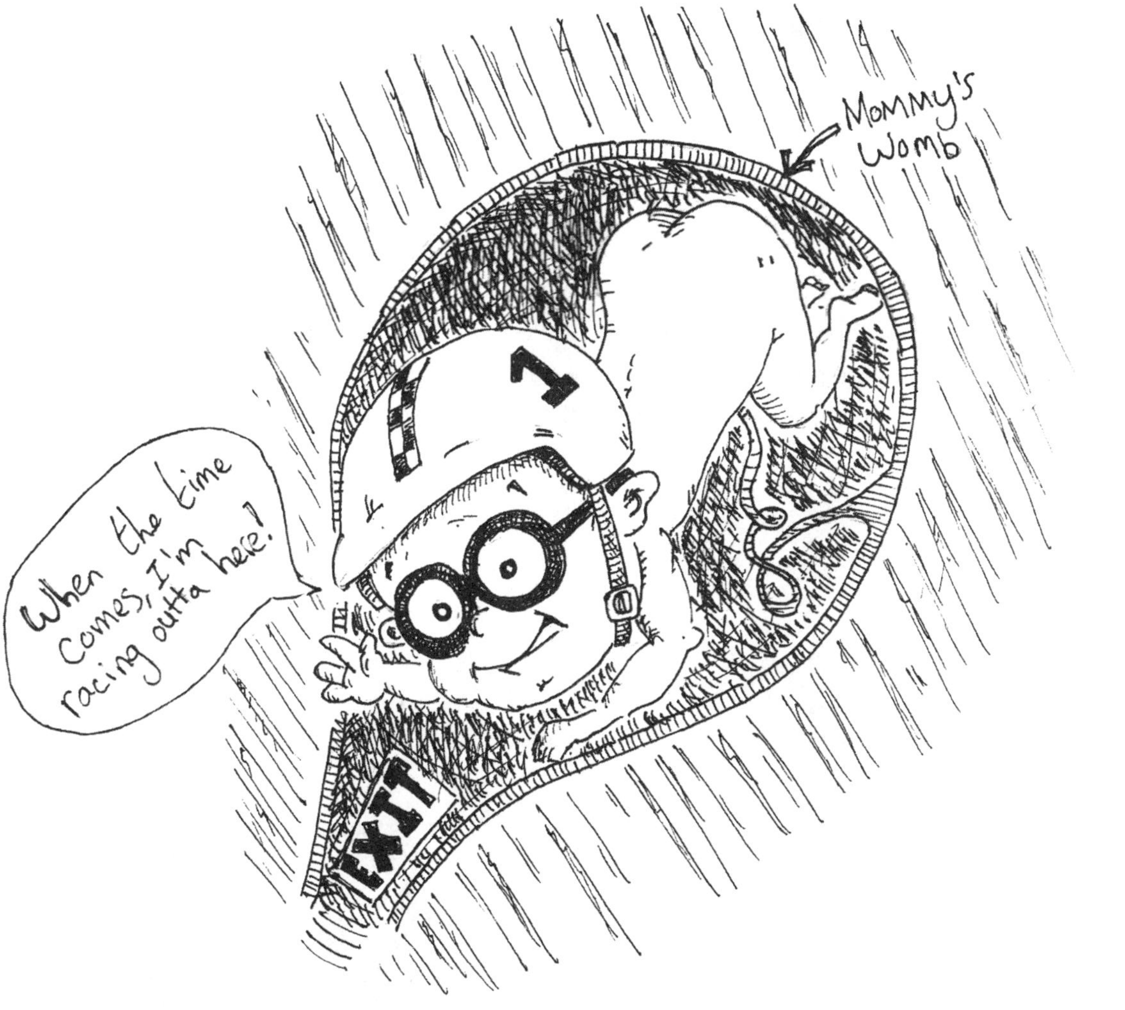
Mommy's Womb
When the time comes, I'm racing outta here!
EXIT

How are babies born?

Most babies around the world are born through their mothers' vagina or middle hole. This is known as natural childbirth. When the baby is fully grown, and there is no more space for it to move inside the womb, it turns with its head facing downwards and its bottom upwards, and it is ready to be born. The entrance to the mother's womb, the cervix, which has been tightly shut throughout the pregnancy to keep the baby safely inside, opens up. It stretches like elastic until it is wide enough for the baby's head to fit through.

So that's how it's done

The baby travels down the vagina head first, and comes out through the woman's middle hole or vaginal opening. The mother's body helps the baby by way of strong muscle cramps called contractions, which push the baby out. First the head comes out, then the shoulders, followed by the rest of the baby's body. It can be quite uncomfortable and even painful for the mother, but it doesn't last for long. After the baby is born, the mother's body releases the placenta and the delivery process is complete.

What is a Caesarean?

Some babies are not born naturally but are removed from their mother's body by way of an operation called a Caesarean section. This is commonly called a Caesar. A Caesar is performed by a special doctor called an obstetrician, who performs an operation and removes the baby through a cut in the lower part of the mother's stomach. The mother is given an anaesthetic, which is a special medical drug that ensures that she feels no pain during the operation.

Some mothers choose to have their babies delivered via Caesarean. Many premature babies (the ones that are born early) enter the world this way. In cases where a mother's body has difficulty giving birth to a baby, endangering her life or the baby's, a Caesar can also be performed. Caesareans can save lives. They are performed in a sterile operating theatre in a hospital.

How are belly buttons made?

Belly buttons are formed when the umbilical cord, which connects the mother to her baby, is cut a few minutes after the baby is born. This does not hurt. The little stump of umbilical cord that is left on the baby's body dries up after a few days and falls off, leaving a belly button.

A midwife, or a special doctor called an obstetrician, usually helps the mother and baby during the birth, whether it is a natural childbirth or a Caesarean. They cut the umbilical cord to separate the baby from its mother because the baby no longer needs the cord to provide it with food, blood and oxygen. After the baby is born and breathing on its own, it gets its food from the milk it sucks from its mother's breast or from a bottle.

What happens next?

Once the umbilical cord has been cut, and the doctor or midwife has checked that the baby and the mother are healthy, the baby is wrapped and usually given to the mother or father. This is a special moment for parents when they see their baby for the first time.

Babies usually cry when they are born because it is a shock to come out of the womb into a world of loud noises, bright lights and fresh air. It is very different from the warm, dark and wet feeling of being inside the womb and the baby is now separated from its mother. When the baby is held by its mother and put to the breast to suckle, it usually calms down very quickly because it feels secure once again.

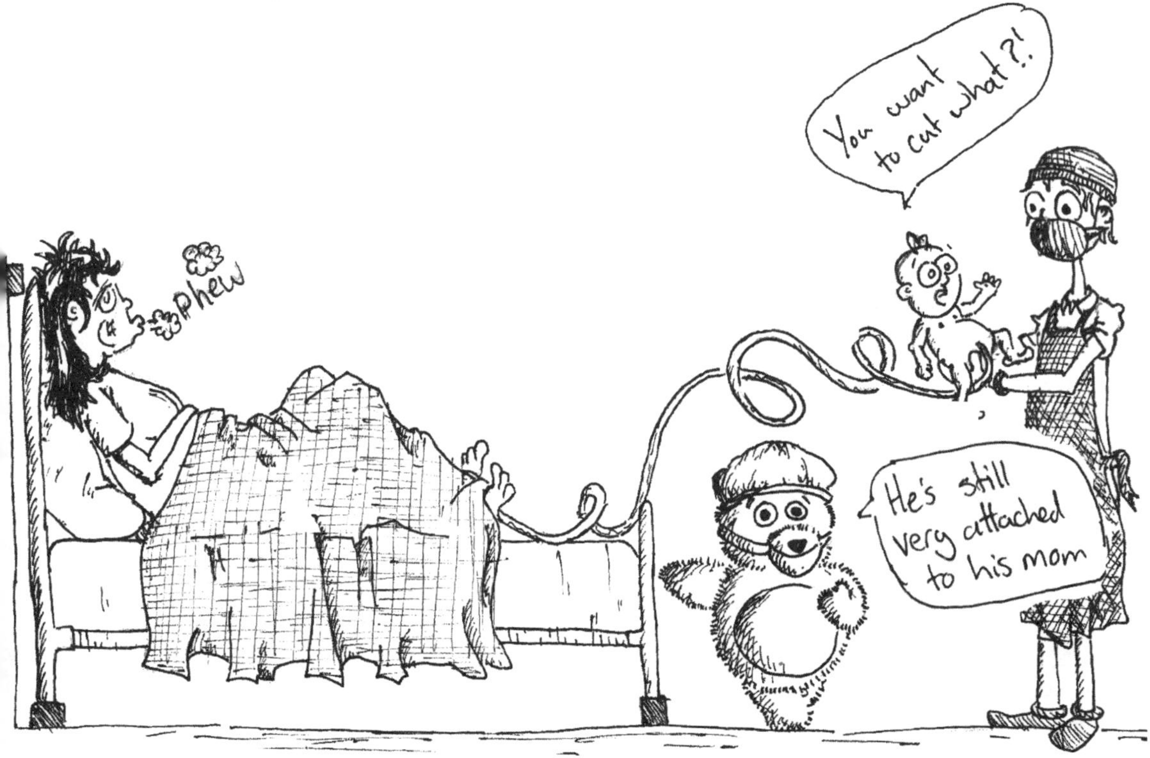
Phew
You want to cut what?!
He's still very attached to his mom

What does the baby eat?

Mothers usually put their new baby to the breast straight after it is born. The baby is happy and content being so close to its mother. When a baby sucks it is very soothing and calms the baby down. Breast milk is the perfect food for a newborn baby, giving it all the goodness it needs to grow strong and healthy. Babies can also be fed with bottles of milk formula. They only start eating real food when they are much bigger.

What happens to the mother's body after pregnancy?

Within a few months after a mother stops breastfeeding her baby, her body shape goes back to normal. Her uterus, which was the size of a large ball during pregnancy, shrinks back to being the size of the mother's fist. Her monthly period will also return which means that she will once again bleed for a few days each month, preparing her uterus for the next pregnancy. Remember that when a woman's periods stop this is one of the signs that she may be pregnant. If a woman does not want to fall pregnant, then she should not have sex, or she should make sure that she and her partner use some form of contraception, such as a condom or The Pill. Contraceptives prevent the sperm from a man from meeting an egg from a woman when they have sex.

easy ANSWERS *to* awkward QUESTIONS

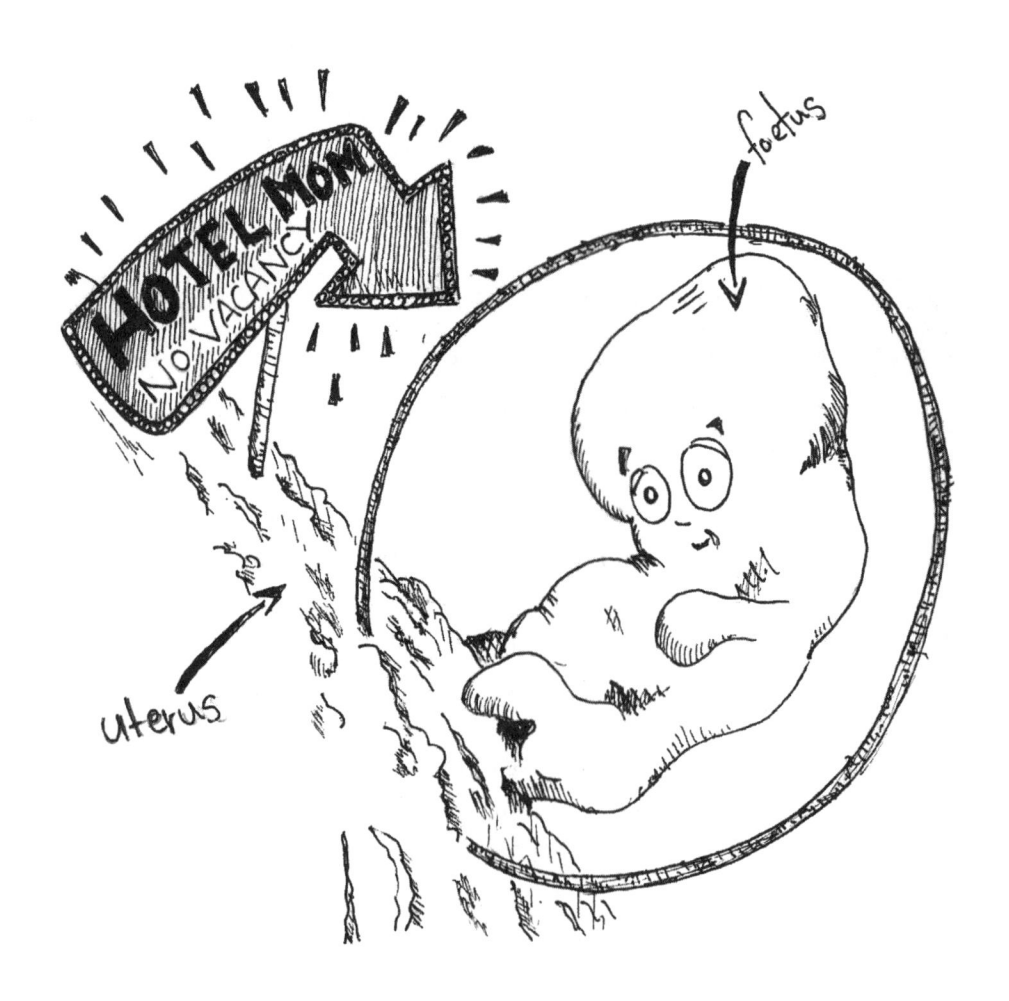

IMPORTANT THINGS TO REMEMBER ABOUT HOW BABIES ARE MADE

- ✔ Never have sex if you are not ready to become a parent.

- ✔ The creation of a baby is one of nature's miracles.

- ✔ The mother's body is able to provide the baby with everything that it needs during the pregnancy and for the first few months of life.

Chapter 7: Words You Need to Understand

CHAPTER 7: Words you need to understand

You listen to the radio, watch the news, read magazines and talk to your friends. You are exposed to a lot of big words with complicated meanings relating to relationships, sex, pregnancy, sexual crimes, sexually transmitted diseases and sexual abuse.

You may think you know what they mean, but just in case you don't, we have created a short dictionary of the most common words or terms you will hear, together with explanations for each one.

Heterosexual relationship

A heterosexual relationship is when a man and a woman, or two people of the opposite sex, love each other and have a relationship with each other. A man and a woman in a heterosexual relationship may have sex with each other if they both want to. When heterosexuals have sex or make love, they rub their private parts together because it makes them feel good, and the man pushes his erect penis inside the woman's vagina or middle hole. It's like two pieces of a jigsaw puzzle fitting together. Sex between a man and a woman can result in pregnancy if a sperm from the man joins together with a woman's egg inside her body. Sperm are released into the woman's vagina through the tip of the man's penis when he ejaculates during sex. An ejaculation is when the penis spurts semen, a whitish liquid containing sperm, during sex. The semen carries the sperm to the woman's egg.

Homosexual relationship

A homosexual relationship is when two people of the same sex, such as two men or two women, fall in love with each other. Homosexual men are often called 'gay' and homosexual woman are usually called 'lesbians'. Homosexuals who love each other can have sex. Sex between homosexuals is different from sex between a man and a woman in a heterosexual relationship.

In a relationship between two gay men, they will hug and kiss each other and they will touch and rub each other's penises. Having sex in this way, in a loving relationship, can make both people feel good. Two lesbian women who love each other will kiss and cuddle each other. They will also touch and rub each other's private parts, including their breasts, vulva, clitoris and vagina. This creates very pleasant feelings in their private parts.

Some people believe it is wrong to be homosexual and other people believe everyone has the right to decide with whom they want to have a relationship. All relationships should be based on love, respect and fairness.

easy ANSWERS to awkward QUESTIONS

Rape

To rape is to force another person to have sex when that person does not want to have sex. To understand this you need to know what healthy sex is. Healthy sex is when the two people who want to have sex together give their permission or consent because they love each other and sex makes them both feel good.

When a person is raped, this is not the case. The person who is being raped or forced to have sex does not feel good. Rape is painful, violent and dangerous. Rape is sex that does not happen in a loving way. The person being raped can be injured physically and emotionally. Rape is wrong. Rape is a crime. People who rape others are called rapists. Rapists who are caught by the police receive a criminal record and are usually sent to prison for a long time. A person who is raped must get help from a doctor and the police immediately. Rape can result in pregnancy, the transmission of sexually transmitted diseases (STDs) and even HIV/AIDS. Both men and women can be raped.

Child abuse

Child abuse is when an adult hurts a child and the child cannot protect him or herself against the adult. There are different forms of abuse: physical, emotional and sexual abuse. Any form of abuse is wrong. When an adult abuses a child, the child must tell someone, such as a parent, teacher, minister/priest, doctor or any adult the child trusts. It is important that someone knows what is happening to you so that they can help you and protect you from harm.

Physical abuse

Physical abuse is when an adult hurts the body of the child. This can be done in many different ways including hitting, kicking, throwing, punching or even burning. It is the adult who is the abuser. It is the adult who has the problem and takes it out on a child without any cause. Children in this situation often feel like they have done something wrong even though this is not true. They feel scared, frightened and unsafe. They no longer trust the adult who is abusing them. It is important for children who are physically abused to get help from someone they trust in order to get them out of this dangerous and sometimes life-threatening situation.

easy ANSWERS to awkward QUESTIONS

Emotional abuse

Emotional abuse is when an adult uses words to hurt a child. The adult says hurtful and harmful things to the child all the time without any cause, making the child feel bad about him or herself. Negative words and phrases are used, such as "You are always in my way!", "You are good for nothing!", "You make me sick!". The abuser may also blame the child for all the problems in the home or swear at him or her. Emotional abuse makes a child feel unsafe and fearful. Emotionally abused children are made to feel as if they have done something wrong when this is not true. They no longer trust the adult, even if it is one of their parents or someone they know. Remember that it is the adult who has the problem and not the child. It is important for the child to get help as soon as possible to stop this very unhealthy situation.

Sexual abuse

Sexual abuse is when an adult uses sex to abuse a child. This can happen in a number of ways:
- The adult may touch the child's private parts.
- The child may be forced to touch the adult's private parts.
- The adult may have sex with the child.
- The adult may photograph or film a child's private parts.

The adult usually threatens the child verbally by telling him or her not to tell anyone about the sexual abuse or they will do something bad to the child or to someone the child loves. Sexually abused children feel very fearful and helpless and think that no one will believe them. Sexual abuse makes children feel very different from their friends. They will try to avoid contact with the adult who is abusing them. Remember that it is the adult who has the problem and not the child. The child is not to blame for being sexually abused. A sexually abused child must tell someone who can help to get him or her out of this very dangerous situation.

Pornography

Pornography includes any images of naked people or people who are having sex. Pornographic material can include photographs, pictures in books or magazines, videos, DVDs, movies or photographs or footage sent via cell phones, email or found on the Internet. Pornography is not for children. It could upset or confuse you because children understand that private parts are private. If anybody shows you pornographic material you should be very alert. Do not stay around, get out as fast as you can and tell a trusted adult. Adults who show children pornographic material often do this before they sexually abuse a child. Someone who looks at pornographic material often can become addicted in the same way as people get addicted to drugs, cigarettes and alcohol. The more they see, the more they want and it can take over their lives.

Sexually transmitted diseases

Sexually Transmitted Diseases (STD) are diseases that affect the private parts – the penis and the vulva, as well as the internal sexual organs of a woman. A person gets infected with an STD when he or she has sex with someone who already has an STD. There are different types of STDs. You may have heard of HIV, AIDS, syphilis, herpes and gonorrhoea, for example. The symptoms of STDs include:
- Sores on the mouth and on the private parts, both inside and outside the body.
- Discharges (oozing) from the private parts.
- Unpleasant smells from the private parts.
- Itching and burning of the private parts.

STDs can make a person feel very sick and must be treated by a medical doctor. In the case of HIV and AIDS, you can die. A person with an STD should never have sex with another person until they are one hundred percent healed and healthy.

HIV and AIDS

HIV stands for Human Immuno Deficiency Virus.
AIDS stands for Acquired Immune Deficiency Syndrome.

HIV is a viral infection that is spread through blood. It is affecting millions of people throughout the world. A person can carry the HIV virus but not be ill. This person would be HIV positive. If they become ill, however, they can get AIDS. AIDS destroys the body's resistance, or ability to fight infection. HIV is spread through unprotected sex. You can also get it from needle stick injuries (pricks from used syringes), or by coming into contact with an infected person's blood through an open sore. Some babies are born with HIV because their mothers were infected. Breast milk can also transfer HIV. You cannot get HIV from hugging, touching, kissing, breathing or sneezing.

AIDS is serious. It makes you very ill and you can die from AIDS. The only way to stop the spread of AIDS is to prevent yourself from getting it. Never touch another person's blood and do not have unprotected sex (this means that a condom must always be used when having sex).

Miscarriage

Babies are created when a man and a woman have sex. When a sperm from a man joins with an egg from a woman, inside her body, this is the beginning of a baby. We say that a woman is pregnant when she is carrying a baby. In the first few months of pregnancy the baby is called a foetus. It doesn't look much like a baby at this stage. Sometimes a woman has a miscarriage in the first few weeks of pregnancy. This is when the foetus dies and is naturally released by the mother's body through the vagina. When this happens, the mother is no longer pregnant. Often there is no explanation as to why this has happened, and at other times there are specific medical reasons for it. When a mother and father have planned a baby and the woman miscarries, they usually feel very sad to have lost their baby.

Abortion

An abortion is different from a miscarriage in that it does not happen naturally. It is when a doctor or medical person removes a foetus, or unborn baby, from a pregnant mother's womb. This usually happens in the early stages of pregnancy for various reasons, such as:

- There may be something medically wrong with the baby.
- This may be an unplanned pregnancy and the parents may feel they are not ready to have a baby yet.
- This may be a teenage pregnancy. Due to the girl's young age she may not want the baby, or it may be dangerous for her to carry the baby because her body is not yet fully developed.
- The pregnancy may be the result of a rape.

Some people believe that abortion is wrong because the foetus is a living being and when it is taken out of the womb it will die. Other people believe every woman has the right to decide whether she wants to have a baby or not. An abortion should only be performed by a qualified medical professional with special sterilised instruments, and in a hygienic room.

Contraceptives

When a woman and a man have sex and they don't want to have a baby, either or both of them should use a contraceptive. There are many different kinds of contraceptives:

- Condoms are a stretchy, thin rubbery cover or "balloon" that a man places over his penis before putting his penis inside a woman's vagina. Use of a condom also helps to prevent the spread of HIV/AIDS and Sexually Transmitted Diseases (STDs), as well as unwanted pregnancies. There is also a female version of the condom that the woman places inside her vagina. It lines the vagina, stopping any of the man's semen from coming into contact with her vagina.
- Condoms are a barrier method of contraception. Others include the diaphragm (a device placed inside the woman's vagina) and spermicidal creams that kill sperm.
- Contraceptive injections or The Pill stop the woman's body from making eggs.
- A device called a loop can be fitted inside a woman's uterus by a medical professional to block the sperm from reaching the egg.
- The best way to avoid having a baby is not to have sex.

IMPORTANT THINGS TO REMEMBER ABOUT YOUR BODY AND FEELINGS

TAKE YOUR BODY SERIOUSLY

One day, when you are older and in a loving relationship, having sex will be one of the ways in which you share your love with another person who loves and respects you. You will feel comfortable and excited about it and it will make you feel happy. Remember that sex is not for children; it is for adults and it can have serious consequences.

Your body is special and belongs to you. You have to look after your body and protect it. Always remember: "My body belongs to me. Nobody is allowed to touch or play with my private parts and I am not to play with, or touch another person's private parts". Protect your body, mind and feelings. You have the right to say "No!" where your body, mind and feelings are concerned.

TRUST YOUR FEELINGS

Your feelings are important and you must learn to trust them and listen to them.

When you feel uncomfortable about anything, your feelings are telling you not to do it or to get help or advice. When you feel embarrassed, this feeling is telling you that you do not feel comfortable with what is happening to you or the situation you are in.

Your feelings are important messengers and they sometimes serve as warnings, guiding you to say "No" to protect yourself. You must listen to your feelings.

INDEX

A
abortion 123
abuse
  child 114
  emotional 117
  physical 115
  sexual 85, 118
adolescent 66
AIDS 68, 85, 113, 121, 124
anus 41

B
babies
  making 90–106
  premature 100
belly buttons 101
birth 98
boys 24–34
  changes 57
  special body parts 25
breast milk 104
breasts 40

C
Caesarean 100
cervix 96
child abuse 114
circumcision 28
conception 76
condoms 83, 124
contraception 83, 124

D
diaphragm 124

E
eggs 79
ejaculate 80
embryo 80
emotional 65
  abuse 117
  changes 54
erection 60

F
family planning 83
feelings 65
foetus 93
foreskin 28

G
girls 38–48
  changes 55
  special body parts 39

H
help 20

heterosexual relationship 111
homosexual relationship 112
hormones 54

I
injections 124

L
labia 40

M
masturbation 15, 45, 62
menstruation 44, 55, 59
miscarriage 122
moody 66

N
nipples 58

O
organisations 20
orgasm 67
ovaries 79

P
penis 25, 78

touching 32
period, *see* menstruation
physical
  abuse 115
  changes 54
Pill, The 83, 124
pornography 119
pregnancy 92, 93, 123
private parts 12, 26
  boy 14
  boys' and girls' 30
  care 31, 46
  girl 14, 40
  touching 15, 16, 18, 19, 33, 47, 118
protection,
  see contraception
puberty 52–70, 54

R
rape 113, 123
reproductive organs 42
rights 8–20

S
scrotum 25, 78
semen 78
sex 67, 69, 74–85

sexual abuse 85, 118
sexually transmitted
  diseases, *see* STD
sperm 25, 78
STD 68, 85, 120, 124

T
testicles 78
touching 15, 16, 18
  penis 32
  vulva 45
  without permission 19, 33, 47, 118
  yourself 62

U
umbilical cord 95, 102
uterus 80

V
vagina 42
vulva 41

W
wet dreams 61